MW01173067

A CHILD'S JOURNEY THROUGH ADOPTION

Michelle Lee Graham

A child's journey through Adoption

Copyright© 2021 Michelle Lee Graham, ALL RIGHTS RESERVED.

No part of this book, or its associated ancillary materials may be reproduced

or transmitted in any form or by any means, electronic or mechanical,

including photocopying, recording, or by any informational storage or

retrieval system without permission from the publisher.

Editor: Alexa Tanen

Illustrator: Yelyzaveta Serdyuk

Format: Rocio Monroy

Photographer: Stephanie Adkisson

To my first grandson, Thomas Jeffrey.

May you always know our story.

The clock said 8:00 pm;
it was my bedtime.
Time to begin our nightly
routine of tuck-ins,
stories, and prayers.

I snuggled into my warm blankets, my mom's loving eyes looking down at me, "Will you tell me, again, how you loved me before you met me?"

I always liked to hear about my adoption story.

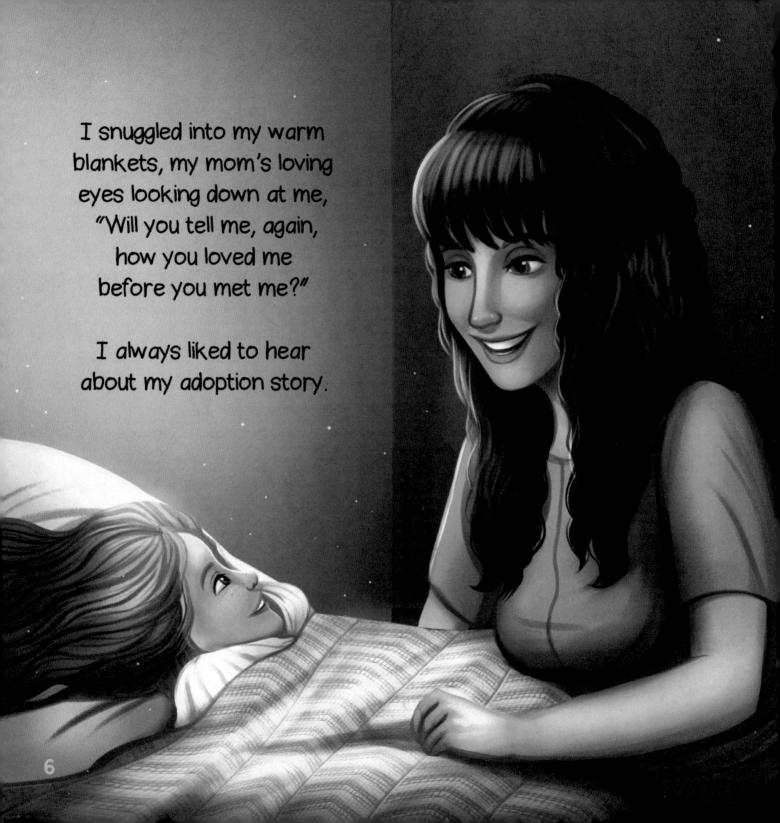

"Once upon a time, before you were born, you grew in another mommy's tummy. You were her first baby and very special to Michelle. She was still very young, but already loved you more than anything."

7

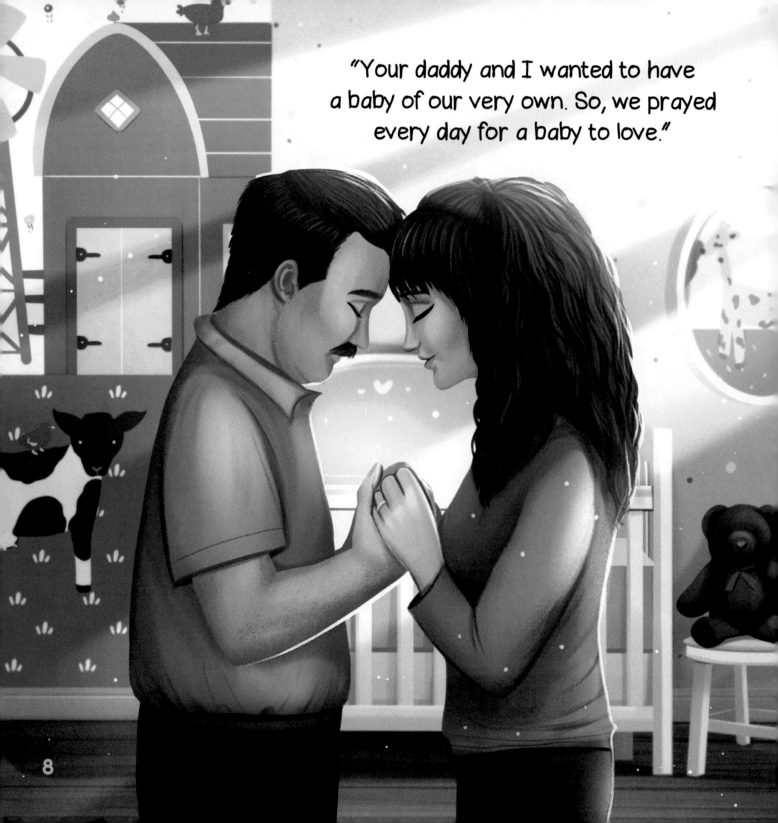

"Your daddy and I wanted to have a baby of our very own. So, we prayed every day for a baby to love."

"At the same time, Michelle searched far and wide for a mom and dad who could give you all you needed. This was her biggest job as your birth mom and, with God's help, we all became family!"

I reached up and grabbed
her neck in a big, warm hug,
"I love you Mommy!"

Later, I learned even more about adoption when
my sister, Lily, was adopted into our family.
I loved becoming
a big sister.

As the years went by, I sometimes wondered about my birth mom and other brothers and sisters. What were they like?

One day I ran across a picture that I had never seen before. It was my birth mom. She actually looked like me. I decided to reach out.

The day I was to arrive, I felt excited.
I knew I was family and would be loved.

Our first visit stretched late into the night. I did not
want to leave and Michelle did not want me to either.
We hugged each other tight.
When it was time to say goodbye, we knew this was
only the beginning of our life together.

As the years have gone by,
I always remember
how much I was loved from
the very beginning of my life.

15

The clock read 8:00 pm; bedtime for Tommy.
Time to begin our nightly routine
of tuck-ins, stories, and prayers.

Tommy snuggled into his warm blankets,
sparkling eyes peeking over the top,
"Mommy, will you tell me a bedtime story?"

I paused for a brief moment, and with a gentle smile, I began...
"Once upon a time, before you and I were born,
Grammy and Grandpa had been praying
for a baby of their very own..."

The End

ABOUT THE AUTHOR

"I am proud to be a Birth Mom and share my personal story with you"

http://michelleleegraham.com/

OTHER TITLES BY MICHELLE :

A Birth Mom's Journey Through Adoption. Experience a birth mother's unwavering devotion to her child. Learn how she navigated the years that followed and openly shared her journey through adoption with her family. Witness the culmination of many years of hope and prayer in a reunion that will melt any heart. A mother and daughter bond that withstood the test of time and can never be broken.

OTHER TITLES BY MICHELLE :

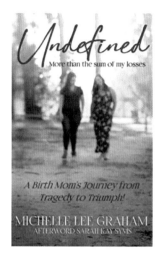

All books are available in Spanish

Available on

Scan the code to get your own copy

Made in the USA
Middletown, DE
10 September 2024

60650131R00015